The Beginner's Guide to Blogging

Nikhil Wad

DEDICATION

To all those lovely people who wish to start their blogging journey, this one is for you.

Like you, I was at this stage where you are now. So, hang in there and keep exploring the opportunities that blogging has to offer.

CONTENTS

ABOUT THE AUTHOR

Nikhil was born and brought up in Mumbai. He has a Diploma in Applied Arts. He is now a social media professional & a content marketer by profession.

He started his career as a graphic designer/ visualizer & after having a decent amount of experience in advertising agencies, he made a switch to social media marketing which indeed had caught his attention during its early days.

To know more about him, visit https://www.nikhilwad.one

1

WHAT IS A BLOG?

A blog is a discussion or informational website published on the World Wide Web consisting of discrete, often informal diary-style text entries (posts). Posts are typically displayed in reverse chronological order, so that the most recent post appears first, at the top of the web page.

Until 2009, blogs were usually the work of a single individual, occasionally of a small group, and often covered a single subject or topic.

In the 2010s, "multi-author blogs" (MABs) emerged, featuring the writing of multiple authors and sometimes professionally edited. MABs from newspapers, other media outlets, universities, think tanks, advocacy groups, and similar institutions account for an increasing quantity of blog traffic.

The rise of Twitter and other "microblogging" systems helps integrate MABs and single-author blogs into the news media. A blog can also be used as a verb, meaning to maintain or add content to a blog.

Many blogs provide commentary on a particular subject or topic, ranging from politics to sports. Others function as more personal online diaries or online brand advertising of a particular individual or company.

A typical blog combines text, digital images, and links to other blogs, web pages, and other media related to its topic. The ability of readers to leave publicly viewable comments, and interact with other commenters, is an important contribution to the popularity of many blogs.

2

WHAT IS THE PURPOSE OF A BLOG?

Some people blog for hobbies, some people blog to earn money, and some others to grow their existing business.

The purpose of blogging will vary from person to person.

HubSpot's study revealed that "53% of marketers say blogging is their top content marketing priority".

Why is blogging even such a big deal?

The main reason for this is – blogging is an inbound marketing channel. The highly targeted people who are already interested in your industry will be visiting your website. It does not involve guesswork you proactively reach out to prospects and hopefully develop interest.

That's the power of a blog.

Share your message

Blogging is a great medium wherein you can share your message or knowledge with the world.

Initially, blogs were just treated as online journals consisting of personal stories, lessons, and experiences. Some people started blogging just like one of their favourite past-time activities.

Later as people realized that blogging can drive targeted traffic through search engines, they thought of treating blogging as a business. This gave rise to a new breed of professional bloggers, who liked to start their business out of blogging.

Blogging as a business

As blogging drives hyper-targeted traffic to your content, you can effectively monetize your blog by making use of contextual ad networks like Google AdSense and also promote your affiliate products.

Succeeding in blogging is all about the demand-supply game.

You need to be in a niche and publish content on topics where there is a lot of demand for content but a low supply of content.

Blogging also gave rise to digital nomads who have a virtual team, and blog from anywhere in the world.

Many travel bloggers are just travelling the world, blogging about it, and getting paid for it.

When you are treating blogging as your business, you need to remember these things:

You need to publish high-quality relevant content.

You should not depend on only one source of income and traffic.

You need to start building your other digital assets as well as your social media profiles, YouTube channel, etc.

You need to remember that blogging is a macro game – purpose + passion + persistence = success.

Blogging to grow your business and brand

Companies are also leveraging blogging and content marketing to drive consistent high-quality leads to their business.

If you already have a website for your brand, chances are there that you don't have a blog. By providing free content on your blog, you can attract a high-quality relevant audience to your website. When these people start reading the content, the brand's blog content strategically builds brand awareness. With this, they likely choose your business over your competitors when faced with options.

You can easily make the competition irrelevant. You can also consider having a lead generation form that gives people a free ebook, a course, a webinar, free consultation in turn for their email addresses. With this lead magnet strategy, you can get more leads for your business.

As these audiences are hyper-targeted who were searching for a specific thing on Google, they likely convert well. Brands like Zendesk, Drift, Evernote, Buffer, Leadpages, and much more attributed their disproportionate success to the power of blogging and content marketing.

If you have any business, I'm sure you have a lead generation strategy in place or maybe even a sales funnel in place. If you consider leveraging blogging to drive qualified leads to the top of your funnel or sales pipeline, you could see wonders and also shave off your large marketing budgets.

All you need to do is publish 2-3 high-quality pieces of content on your blog every week. You can do it initially by blog outsourcing or having a content team.

Build a portfolio

If you are a freelance writer, programmer, designer, or do any online work, you need to consider having a portfolio website for showcasing your work.

People when they see you have a real website, with proven work, they are more likely to hire you for their next projects. Along with this, you need to also have your blog content, which proves the fact that you are passionate about the field you are serving.

For example, if you are a freelance writer you can have content that helps other writers. When your prospect clients notice that you are guiding other freelance writers, being yourself a freelancer they'll more likely hire you! I would say, rather than having a resume, you need to consider having your website and a blog.

Personal branding

I would say personal branding is the undeniable reason why you need to blog.

Moving forward in this information age, you'll see personal branding (a brand built around you as a person) matters a lot when it comes to landing a lucrative job, getting more clients, getting recognition, etc.

Personal branding is becoming crucial in areas like expert training and also for marketing agencies.

Although you can build your brand on social media, YouTube, and other channels having your website with your blog is a must.

3

WHAT IS A BLOGGING PLATFORM?

A blogging platform is a software or service used to manage and publish content on the internet in the form of a blog. A blog—short for weblog—is a record of a user's entries online, usually in reverse chronological order.

A blogging platform allows the user to create, organize, and publish written and visual content online in a blog.

The primary thing that distinguishes a blog from other websites is that the content that is published onto a blog is shown in reverse chronological order, meaning that the most frequent additions to the website are shown first.

Blogging platforms allow the user to publish a post, display the date that the post was published, and assign a specific author assigned to the post. These software or web-based services also allow users to tag content with specific categories, making it easier to search for all posts on-topic within the blog. These platforms also allow users to tag posts with multiple keywords as another way to search for specific topics.

One of the advantages of using a blogging platform is that it makes optimizing your blog for the search engines easy to do. Most blogging platforms will have fields for you to include metadata, which helps tell the search engines what your website is about. This information usually includes a title for your page, a description of your post, and some related keywords.

4

LIST OF BLOGGING PLATFORMS

Choosing the right platform will play a vital role in achieving your blogging goals.

It's always best to go with a blogging platform that's easy to set up, and won't require any coding skills. You'll also need to think about what kind of blog you want to create, now and in the future.

As your blog grows, you may want to change the look of your blog and add more features for your growing audience. That means it's important to choose a flexible blogging platform, with room to grow.

Here are some of the well-known platforms which you can explore:

WordPress

It comes in two variations. WordPress.com & WordPress.org.

WordPress.com is the variation wherein one can start the blog on the WordPress server itself and also is the least expensive option. If you are an entry-level blogger, start with WordPress.com.

But if you wish to take your blogging to a whole new level & are looking to gain leverage from your blogging then go for WordPress.org wherein one can install WordPress on the user's server. Though when it comes to WordPress.org, one is liable to set a web hosting account & a domain name for the blog to setup & to make it active. The advantage of the same is that all the content remains on the user-owned hosting server.

Blogger

It's the most popular platform provided by Google.

The advantage of having the blog on Blogger is that it comes with SEO benefits by default. Most personal bloggers prefer this option. It lacks the freedom of customization but the advantage is that the blogs get indexed real quick on Google.

Squarespace

It's one of the premium blogging platforms wherein they do not provide any free plans but the interface, user-experience is worth it & their CMS give the liberty to play with the templates the way you would like.

They do provide a 14-day trial service. They also have the eCommerce option available for those who are looking forward to selling their products online.

Wix

Their powerful technology allows everyone to get online with a stunning, professional and functional web presence.

Whether it's your first time creating or you're a long-time expert, you'll find the features and solutions you need to build a professional website with true creative freedom.

They have the most economical plans when it comes to their subscription.

Shopify

I won't say Shopify is a blogging platform, it is more of an eCommerce platform.

But their themes do include blogging features wherein you can publish blog posts. Opt for this platform only if your main priority is to build an eCommerce website for your products, courses etc.

5

HOW TO CHOOSE THE PERFECT NICHE FOR YOUR BLOG?

What is a niche?

It's basically what your blog will be about.

Starting a blog can be challenging if you are unable to find your niche. And it's best to narrow down to your niche before you proceed with finalizing your domain name & web hosting for the blog.

Ask yourself questions like:

What do you want to write about?

What is it that you want to share with the audience?

What is your passion?

Do you have a special field of expertise?

What could you write about basically forever?

You must be knowing better about what you are good at. Either go for a broad niche or a tight one.

List down all the topics you would want to focus on & then go for the final topic selection out of those options.

To help you identify your niche, here are some options you can explore:

City guide and information

Travel guide and tips

Language

Health and fitness

Mental health and selfcare

Beauty and skincare

Gardening

Art

Music reviews

Movie reviews

Television show reviews

Technology

Gadget

Design

Web Development and programming

Photography

Fashion

Cooking and baking

Food reviews

Finance, insurance and investments

Parenting

News and current events

Sports

Hobbies

Personal (This & that)

Important factors to consider while choosing the right blog niche:

Though there is no perfect niche, while choosing the right niche for your blog, you should consider these three important factors.

Passion

The very first factor which matters the most while choosing the right niche for your blog is your passion.

How passionate you are about something?

What is the one thing you love doing the most?

What is something you keep talking about the whole day and doesn't get tired of?

The key is to find out something you don't want to take a vacation from. If you can find something in you then you would be able to create and share valuable content consistently around that topic with full energy, enthusiasm. This will result in better user engagement.

Knowledge

The next factor is your knowledge.

What do you know about something?

How much knowledge do you have in that niche?

Are you willing to learn more about the same topic?

The key is here to share your knowledge with your audience that adds some value to their life.

Potential

Finally, you need to analyze the potential in that particular niche.

Is there sufficient demand for the topic you are going to blog about?

Are there content creators in that niche?

If there is enough demand and some bloggers are making a decent amount of money in the same niche then you are ready to go. Competitors are your biggest source of learning, remember that.

Everything comes down to research. Robust research is the key.

Competitive Analysis

Competitive analysis is one of the effective strategies to choose the right niche for you. You can do some competitive research by exploring some of the top blogs in your niche. That will help you to track how much traffic they are getting on their blogs and at the same time, you can analyze how they are monetizing their blogs. Moreover, you can also dig into their income reports where they share the amount of money that they made along with their different sources of income in detail.

Keyword Research based on your niche

You should start by searching on the broad niche as well as the narrow niches. Let's say you want to start a blog on digital marketing. So, you can search for "digital marketing", "social media marketing", "email marketing" and so on.

You can use some keywords research tools like Ubersuggest. You can also check SEMrush, Ahrefs which are some of the best SEO tools with a huge database for better accuracy.

By doing so, you can easily track what is search volume on these keywords. If there is a search volume of more than 10,000 per month for a broad niche then it's good to go.

Check affiliate products in your niche

Next, you should check for affiliate products in your niche. Affiliate marketing is one of the biggest sources of making money online. So whichever niche you choose you should explore for affiliate products to promote on your website.

Some frequently asked questions about niche…

Does your blog need a niche?

Yes, to run a successful blog you need to choose a specific niche for your blog. A specific blog niche will help you to bring targeted traffic, create authority sites faster, and results in better profitability.

How do you choose a profitable niche?

Your passion, knowledge, and niche potential are three primary factors to choose a profitable niche for your blog.

What blog niches are most profitable?

Finance, Health, Fitness, Travel, Lifestyle, Tech, Online Money-Making Blogs, to name a few.

What should I blog about?

Based on your passion and knowledge you can start a blog around Traveling, Health, Fitness and sports, Food, Entertainment, Gaming, Finance, and so on.

Which niche makes the most money on YouTube?

Beauty/Fashion, Gaming, Food/Cooking, Fitness/Health, Unboxing/Reviews, Travel, Pets/Animal, Humour, Entertainment, Vlogs/Storytimes, are some of the best niches on YouTube that makes the most money.

6

DON'T UNDERESTIMATE THE POWER OF A DOMAIN NAME

The domain name will give an online identity to your blog.

Once you are done with finalizing your blogging niche, the very next step is to narrow down the name of your blog which will also eventually be the domain name. When I had decided to choose a domain name for my blog, I did go through a lot of confusion & dilemma in just narrowing it down to one.

Before choosing the domain name, make sure you are happy with the name of your blog.

THINGS TO CONSIDER WHEN CHOOSING A DOMAIN NAME

Make sure it is easy to remember and is short.

The domain name should always be easy to remember & should make sense too. And not to forget, to keep it short & sweet to sound catchy.

Do not use hyphens or symbols.

Using hyphens & symbols will not only give an odd visual appeal to the domain name but will also be a turn-off for some people.

Take some time in picking the right extension. We are lucky to have several domain extensions options available for us these days. Be it country-specific or business-specific, the list goes on & on. But extensions such as .com, .net, .info, .biz etc. are mostly preferred by many. Yet, .com tops the charts. It solely depends on what your focus of the blog will be.

It should be related.

No matter what, always go for a name that will relate to your blog. If it's a personal blog, go for your name. My advice will be that always take some time in narrowing down to the final domain name & make sure you stick to that name!

List down all your options.

Make sure you list down all your domain name combinations. It will be such that most of the domain names won't be available. So, my suggestion will be to make a list of 7-10 variations of your domain name.

CHOOSING THE RIGHT WEB HOSTING SERVICE IS ESSENTIAL

...only if you are going for a self-hosted WordPress option for your blog.

A trusted & reliable web hosting service will make sure that your blog stays live throughout its course & never be unavailable for your valuable readers.

GoDaddy was recommended by several people. Choosing a web hosting platform will depend upon your requirement & how you adapt to their interface.

Apart from GoDaddy, you might also want to look at Bluehost, HostGator.

But...

If you are going for Blogger, Wix, Squarespace or Shopify, you won't need a web-hosting service.

Though, you will have to subscribe to a paid plan of Wix, Squarespace or Shopify, whereas, Blogger is completely free and you only will have to link your domain to your blog.

9

AN INCREASE IN BLOG TRAFFIC LEADS TO SEVERAL OPPORTUNITIES

No matter how much traffic you will get, that will always feel less.

Don't underestimate the power of social media. Your main source of blog traffic would come from social media, especially Twitter, Facebook & Linkedin.

Make sure you share your blog posts more than once on your social platforms & that too at different time zones.

Few social media scheduling services like Buffer, Meet Edgar will be of great support.

On Twitter, it's okay to post multiple times but make sure your tweet copy is not the same. Bring variations to your context. Join blogging communities, groups on Facebook, be a part of Twitter chats related to blogging.

This will help you to reach out to other bloggers & build a network.

Another way of increasing your blog traffic is by implementing a robust search engine optimization strategy. In short, you will have to optimize your blog posts with right and high-ranking keywords so that your blog will start ranking on Google for those specific keywords.

10

MAINTAINING CONSISTENCY IN PUBLISHING POSTS IS IMPORTANT

It's very important to maintain a publishing schedule to attract readers to your blog.

You don't want your blog visitors to come to your blog & see no posts at all or a post that was published several months back. The next very moment they are going to move away without reading your posts.

To keep your blog visitors interested, you will need to be consistent with your publishing schedule. To begin with 2 blog posts a month is not a bad idea. Depending on your niche/ genre you can tweak your publishing schedule.

.

11

MAKE MONEY FROM BLOGGING

Yes, your blog can be a sweet source of revenue for you. It takes time to build a decent amount of income from the blog & it does not happen overnight.

You want to make money, right? Of course, you do.

Everyone wants – and needs to make money.

So, you started a blog since you've heard it's an easy way to make cash, but you're not quite sure how to make money doing it. Or maybe you already have a blog and you're exploring ways to monetize it.

No matter which group you're in, making money with a blog – whether it's a hobby blog or a business blog –is possible. It's not a get rich quick ordeal, but if you do it right, you could make enough to support your family and more.

Monetize with CPC or CPM ads

One of the most common ways bloggers make money is through placing ads on the website.

There are two popular types of ads.

CPC/PPC Ads: Cost per click (also called pay per click) ads are usually banners that you place in your content or sidebar. Each time a reader clicks on the ad, you are paid for that click.

CPM Ads: CPM Ads, or "cost per 1,000 impressions," are ads that pay you a fixed amount of money based on how many people view your ad.

Perhaps the most popular network for placing these types of ads is Google AdSense. With this program, you do not need to be in direct contact with advertisers; you simply place the banner on your site, Google chooses ads relevant to your content, and your viewers click on the ads.

Sell private ads

Working with advertising networks isn't your only option when it comes to selling ads. If you end up with enough traffic, advertisers may come directly to you and ask you to place their ad on your website.

You can also contact advertisers yourself.

The biggest difference from the above-mentioned option is that there is no middle man, which means you can set your ad rates. Selling private ads can come in the form of banners, buttons, or links.

You can even make money writing sponsored posts where you write about or give a review of an advertiser's product or service.

Another option is to write an underwritten post or series, which is where you can write about any topic, but the advertiser pays for a "Brought to you by" mention in the content.

The ways you make money with this can vary. For instance, you might charge a one-time fee for a link within a post. If you are hosting banner ads, you might charge your partner monthly.

Include affiliate links in your content

Affiliate marketing is also another great tool for monetizing your blog.

Here is how affiliate marketing works: An advertiser has a product she wants to sell. She agrees to give you a commission from each sale if the buyer is coming from your site. She gives you a unique link that tracks your affiliate code. That way, she knows when a buyer used your link to make a purchase. You include your affiliate link on your website.

You can do this directly in the content or through banner ads. If a reader clicks on your unique link and buys the product you have recommended, you earn a percentage of what she purchased.

You can utilize affiliate marketing through ad networks like Amazon Associates, or you can create private partnerships with advertisers and businesses with an affiliate program.

Sell digital products

If you would rather not advertise other people's products on your site, or if you are looking for another stream of income, consider selling digital products.

This can include items like eBooks Online courses/workshops images, video, or music people can use in their content apps, plugins, or themes.

Just remember that if you are going to choose one of these avenues that you make it relevant and useful to your readers.

A lot of bloggers make the mistake of assuming they are developing a product their readers need; listen to your readers first, and then create a digital product that will meet their needs.

Use it as a content marketing tool for your business

It is also possible to sell physical products on your blog and to make money that way.

Instead of thinking of it as making money from your blog, however, think of your blog as a content marketing tool that will drive visitors to your business website.

The possibilities are practically endless when it comes to developing a business blog. You could sell hand-made products, books, manufactured products, and so much more. Or you might already have a business and decide to start a blog to convert loyal customers.

Sell memberships

Another option to make money is to sell memberships to exclusive corners of your website.

For instance, a career blog might charge $9.99 per month for users to gain access to their job board.

A startup business blog might sell memberships to their forums where people can get personalized advice about their business.

The key here is that your exclusive membership has to be more valuable than something your visitors can find for free somewhere else, so be sure you're developing something of value and worth the price.

Use it to build your credibility

Blogging to build credibility can lead to many money-making opportunities. For instance, let us say you start a blog in the finance industry.

People start reading your content, and your blog becomes very popular. You are now a recognized figure in the finance industry. Once you have that authority, people might approach you to co-author a book on debt management, or you could charge to speak at conferences or to run employee financial training days.

This certainly isn't a direct form of making money blogging, but it has worked for many well-known bloggers, and it can work for you, too. If you're looking for a direct revenue stream, popular blogs have sold for 4-7 figures (sometimes more) by selling their branding and content. The biggest thing to keep in mind is that making money blogging is not possible by putting your site up and letting it sit there.

The "if you build it, they will come" mentality doesn't work here, so be sure you're willing to put in the time. Most bloggers don't see a spike in income for several months (sometimes years) after starting their blog.

Before you dive too deep into blogging, remember these little bits of advice:

Create quality content

You are not going to make any money from your blog if people don't read it. After all, your readers are the ones who are going to make you money, whether they're clicking on your ads or buying your products. Always put your readers first.

Don't spend your time exclusively on your blog

Developing a successful blog has a lot to do with building relationships. That can include relationships with sponsors, affiliate partners, or simply other bloggers who will direct traffic to your blog. Be sure some of your time is spent on forums and other blogs (or whatever works for you) to build these relationships and your blog.

Don't be afraid to experiment

Not all of these tips and avenues of income are going to work for you. Don't be afraid to tweak your methods to see what works best for you and your readers.

Making money blogging can take a lot of persistence, but it can pay off in the long run if you're starting from scratch.

Just remember that you don't have to use all of these money-making avenues at once. Consider what other people in your industry are doing, and start from there.

Over time, you will learn what works for you and what doesn't.

Thank you for reading!

Printed in Great Britain
by Amazon

21644598R10020